Transforming Medicine and Business with Biblical Principles

Examples of Joseph Lister and John Wanamaker

The Law of God — Our Life and Standard

The Bible repeatedly declares that God's law-word is to be central in our life and society. To the extent that it is, things will go well for us. Deuteronomy 5:29 states: "Oh, that they had such a heart in them that they would fear Me and always keep all My commandments, that it might be well with them and with their children forever!"

This is God's heart for us today, yet, too many of those who call Him Lord live in a different reality — that stated in Jeremiah 7: 23-24:

> But this is what I commanded them saying, "Obey My voice, and I will be your God, and you will be My people; and you will walk in all the way which I commanded you, that it may be well with you." Yet they did not obey or incline their ear, but walked in their own counsels and in the stubbornness of their evil heart, and went backward and not forward.

We have two options for our life. One, look to God as the source of truth and how to live our lives, obey what He commanded, and it will be well. Two, look to ourselves, to man or the state as the source of how to live, and walk accordingly. The result of this is that man will go backward. The latter describes the situation in the world today, but, sadly, it also describes the situation in much of the church. It describes as well the situation in the marketplace.

If we obey God's law, we will be blessed. If we disobey we will be cursed. This message is repeated more than any other message in the Bible.

As we apply His word, His government (or kingdom) comes to our lives, our families, our businesses, our nations, and to the earth. It goes well when this occurs. His Word speaks to all of life. God's law brings life in many areas, touching all aspects of life that are needed today, such as: principles of warfare, penalties of criminals, laws of restitution, laws for provision for the poor, principles of taxation, principles of land usage, principles of building safe buildings, laws of cleanliness and sanitation.

Occupying through Our Occupation

Jesus taught that we are to occupy until He returns (Luke 19:11 ff). It is through our occupation that this will be carried out in a large degree. We must apply His Word to our occupation in order for us (and it) to succeed in fulfilling His desire of advancing His Kingdom in the earth.

God gave us His all-encompassing laws for our good. A study of the application of these laws in nations at various times in history reveals the blessings that God promised do come when we obey. These blessings are seen in the areas of civil and religious liberty, government, economics, business, and the medical field. Through applying Biblical principles of cleanliness, quarantine, and sanitation, Dr. Joseph Lister instituted a new era in the field of medicine, saved millions of lives, and brought an untold benefit to mankind.

Joseph Lister, Founder of Antiseptic Surgery

The great accomplishments of Joseph Lister came about because he applied Biblical medical principles. The laws of God he applied included:

1. Cleanliness — cleansing after contact with those who have died (Num. 19:11-22; see also Num. 9:10; and scriptures given below). Aspects of these laws included:

- A person was unclean for 7 days if he touched a dead body, in a field or in a tent.
- The unclean person was to wash in running water twice during the week (Num. 19:7, 12).
- If someone died in a tent, whoever was in the tent or anyone entering the tent was unclean for 7 days, and every open vessel with no cover was unclean (Num. 19:15). [Lister did experiments showing that germs travel on dust in the air. God, of course, knew this, which is reflected in the Mosaic laws given to man thousands of years earlier.]
- Clothes were to be washed, as well as things made of wood, leather, etc. (Num. 31:19-20).
- If a person touched a dead animal he was also unclean (Lev. 5:2-3; 11:8).

Thus, separation from death was required of God's people. This was symbolic as well as for practical health reasons.

Failure to adhere to God's cleanliness principles is why 10% of pregnant women who went to hospitals in Europe in the middle 1800s to be examined died. Doctors went from doing autopsies to examining the women without washing.

2. Sanitation — cover excrement to prohibit spread of germs (Deut. 23:9-14).

Failure to adhere to this precept led to the Black Death spreading throughout Europe and killing tens of millions in 1348 and the few years following.

3. Quarantine — (Deut. 24:8; Lev. 13-15 [leprosy in the Bible included a variety of infectious diseases])

The laws of quarantine are an application of the sixth commandment, "you shall not murder," with its positive corollary to preserve and further life. Some aspects of these laws included:

- Isolation of the infected person occurs as the disease was evaluated to see if it was contagious (Lev. 13:4, 5, 21, 26, 31, 33).
- If the disease was seen to not be contagious, he was to wash his clothes and be clean (Lev. 13:6, 34).
- If it was contagious, then the person was to live in isolation outside the camp (Lev. 46).

Lister Fulfills His Holy Calling

Joseph Lister was born in England in 1827 in a Christian (Quaker) home. The desires, skills, and character to be a surgeon were implanted in him from a young age. It was no surprise he pursued this study in college. While at University College he learned of the harsh realities of being a surgeon at this time. Infection and death were an everyday occurrence in the surgeon wards. About one out of every three people who underwent amputation died of a wound infection. As a medical student visiting the surgical wards, Lister heard the cries of patients, smelled the fetid odor of festering wounds, and observed the great number of deaths that were typical in that day. Surgery was a difficult and challenging profession, and was not held in high esteem in the medical field. Nonetheless, after four years of study, Lister took his Bachelor of Medicine in 1852 and passed the examinations for admission to the Royal College of Surgeons of England.

"A Glorious Occupation"

At the beginning of 1857, Lister performed his first operation before the students when his boss and mentor, Dr. Syme, was out of town. At this time surgeries were observed by many students as a means of learning. He wrote to his sister of the success of his "debut:"

> The theatre was again well filled, and though I again felt a good deal before the operation, yet I lost all consciousness of the presence of the spectators

during its performance, and did it exactly as if no one had been looking on. I feel, I may say, truly thankful I was able to go through it as I did. Just before the operation began, I recollected that there was only one Spectator whom it was important to consider, One present alike in the operating theatre and in the private room; and this consideration gave me increased firmness. . . .

I trust I may be enabled in the treatment of patients always to act with a single eye to their good, and therefore to the glory of our Heavenly Father. If a man is able to act in this spirit, and is favored to feel something of the sustaining love of God in his work, truly the practice of surgery is a glorious occupation. I may say I never felt better pleased with my profession than now.[1]

Lister recognized that any occupation is glorious if done in a Biblical manner. He understood what Jesus taught, that we are to occupy through our occupation, whether that be in the pulpit ministry, civil ministry, educational profession, medical profession, etc. God has called His people to impact all spheres of life and to use the talents and skills He has given to them to extend His kingdom in the earth.[2] Lister saw his profession as a ministry of God, and he sought to conduct it in a Biblical manner. Lister taught his students that the two great requirements of a physician were "a warm, loving heart and truth in an earnest spirit."[3]

From the beginning of Lister's work as a house surgeon, he had been greatly bothered by the prevalence of wound infection on the surgical wards, which often led to the death of the patient. Witnessing this almost caused him to give up becoming a surgeon. Such infection was also prominent on Syme's wards and his own. This most occurred with those of open wounds, and almost always in those patients who were bedded close to others who had infection. It was as if some kind of poison or something was being transmitted from one patient to another.

Infection was greater in hospital wards than in homes. It would be best for patients to receive treatment and remain at home. But only the more affluent could afford to do so.

Personal cleanliness was not known then as it is today. Baths were taken much less frequently. Hospitals were usually less clean than homes. Surgeons and nurses went from patient to patient without even washing their hands. Surgeons performed operations in blood-stained coats, with the more stains indicative of greater experience. Their instruments were not washed before operations, only afterwards. They knew nothing of germs and how infection or diseases spread. They were not applying God's principles of quarantine or cleanliness. The consequence was much pain, suffering, and death. As mentioned before, about 30% of patients died who were operated on and had open wounds.

Lister insisted upon cleanliness in his wards, requiring everyone to wash before and after treating wounds and to use clean towels. Those with open wounds must have their dressings changed frequently. Many saw this as extravagant, since it required so many clean towels and much effort to wash. Others ridiculed Lister for such action. Some said it was almost profane as he was trying to go against the decrees of the Almighty, who brought infirmity upon those as He willed. With all Lister's efforts, though he saw a little progress, wound infection still remained rampant.

Before anesthesia, surgeons performed operations as rapidly as possible to reduce the time of great pain. This did not allow them to perform delicate, complicated surgeries. Even after anesthesia became common, many surgeons still operated very quickly, to demonstrate their "skills." Lister, though, rejected such thought and over the years performed many complicated and time-consuming operations. While the operations were very successful, and his skills became known to many, a large percentage of his patients still developed gangrene and other infections. He regarded wound infection as "one of the greatest opprobia [disgraces] of modern surgery."[4]

Lister had been conducting experiments to try to discover what caused the infections and had noticed that patients who did not have wounds exposed to the hospital air rarely became infected. He concluded that something in the hospital air caused putrefaction (rotting) of the wound, which was then followed by suppuration (pussiness). But he did not know what this was.

One day his eyes were opened — "something like scales fell from his eyes," in the words of the Bible — as he was reading a publication by a young French chemist. The reason for the putrefaction of wounds became clear to him through the "beautiful researches of Pasteur."[5]

In 1856, Louis Pasteur had discovered that microbes caused fermentation. Living microscopic organisms — germs — were the cause of grape juice fermenting, and of the decomposition of certain substances such as meat. Accompanying this process, which was called putrefaction, was the development of foul-smelling gases. Pasteur showed that germs caused putrefaction. This was the beginning of the most far-reaching scientific development of the nineteenth century. His work revealed why God had given laws of quarantine and cleanliness to mankind. Long before man understood germs, God knew all about them.

Where did these germs originate? Did they come from parent cells or did they spontaneously generate? Many atheistic thinkers had proposed that life sprung from nothing, that there was spontaneous generation. Pasteur's work proved that life can only come from life, no matter how small. All cells stemmed from parent cells. To the Christian thinker, the first cells were created by God, they did not come from nothing. He was the first life source.

Lister Applies Germ Theory to Surgery

Now that Lister knew that germs caused infection in patients, he knew what to attack. If he could prevent germs from getting into wounds, or kill them if they were there, he could stop the dreadful effects of their infection. He would devote the rest of his life to this treatment, but he would encounter many difficulties along the way.

In looking for an agent to kill germs Lister tried carbolic acid, which was discovered in the 1830s and had been used with success in treating sewage. He, of course, was looking for something that would not only kill germs but do so without damaging human tissue. The first patient upon whom Lister tried "antiseptic treatment," was a man with a compound fracture. This attempt, in March of 1865, was not a success. It was months later before he was able to try this treatment again. A boy run over by a cart had a compound fracture with a large, deep wound. After setting the bone, Lister bandaged the leg with a diluted solution of carbolic acid. He was very careful to keep the wound bandaged for many days, well beyond the time where wounds would become infected. This boy healed without any major infection, which usually accompanied such wounds. While encouraged, Lister knew this was not proof, for it could be that it would have healed on its own. A third attempt using this new antiseptic treatment was a semi-failure. After nine months he had no real knowledge of its usefulness.

In 1866 he had seven cases of compound fractures where he treated the patients with antiseptics. All had been severely injured. None developed great infection and none had to have their limbs amputated. Such success had not been seen before, and to Lister it was beyond chance. He reported his results in a major medical journal called the *Lancet*. He was presenting evidence that would revolutionize surgery forever. Yet, he was to discover the great difficulty men have had throughout history of introducing new ideas into various fields. Most physicians paid little attention to his new ideas. Some even attacked him, saying his theories were ridiculous. Lister had discovered a new principle — that germs are a cause of disease — but few people would even listen to him. It would take many years of suffering much ridicule before this began to change.

Lister continued treating wounds and also set out to show through many experiments that there are microscopic germs that cause putrefaction. Even though these were successful and presented strong evidence, English surgeons were slow to believe. Many would not even consider his teachings.

Before Lister's antiseptic treatment, hospitals were commonly places of much infection and suffering. As Lister began to apply principles of cleanliness and his antiseptic system of treatment, the hospital ward of the Royal Infirmary that he oversaw became the most healthy of any ward in the world. He published a paper, entitled "On the Effects of the Antiseptic System of Treatment upon the Salubrity [healthfulness] of a Surgical Hospital," presenting the dramatic effects. Before antiseptic treatment his patients had suffered from all the typical hospital diseases; yet, in the first nine months after introducing the new treatment, he had not had one case of gangrene, blood poisoning (pyemia), or erysipelas. In the years that followed he saw only an occasional case of infection.

His work would transform surgery, as his students recognized, writing, "Your method of Antiseptic Treatment constitutes a well-marked epoch in the history of British Surgery, and will result in lasting glory to the Profession, and unspeakable benefit to mankind."[6] Though this was true, he would experience strong opposition for years to come. But his determination and Christian character would sustain him as he pursued, what he said was, his "noble and holy calling." A former critic, Professor Wood, said of Lister:

> I do not know which to admire more — the scientific mind which has grasped a great principle and applied it, or the character of the man who has unswervingly pursued the object of his life, patiently perfecting, one by one, the means adapted to procure the end in view.[7]

Lister's application of Biblical truth in the medical field brought what God said it would — blessing and life to mankind. This is one of many areas we could examine.[8] The people who have brought blessing, life, advancement, justice, peace, and true wealth, have been those who have applied God's law-word to all areas. The commands of the supreme Law-Giver are true and produce life. We need to learn them and apply them. The result of neglecting God's commands, in whatever area, is decay and death.

John Wanamaker

A Kingdom Businessman Who Founded Modern Merchant Business

Kingdom businesses are much more than businesses run by Christians with the goal to preach Christ and see people converted. Ken Eldred gives this definition: "Kingdom business is for-profit business ventures designed to facilitate God's transformation of people and nations."[9] What would a Kingdom business look like? Following are ten characteristics of Kingdom business:[10]

Ten Characteristics of Kingdom Business

1. Biblical men, in character and worldview, will provide the vision and direction of the business. They primarily shape the spirit or culture of the business.

The founder(s) of the business first sets this culture, but this must be passed on to all those who become involved in the business and also transferred to future generations. There can be non-Christians who work for a kingdom business, but they will be influenced by the culture of the business, rather than the business being influenced negatively by them. In addition, they should reflect this culture to the customers of the business.

2. The spirit or culture of the business will reflect and emanate Biblical character and truth.

Kingdom business (which includes all the people who are a part of the business) will line up with God's precepts in His Word, including such things as:

- Hard work brings success (Prov. 12:24; 10:4, 5; 14:4).
- Conduct your life and business on Godly morality (Prov. 11:11; 29:18; 28:13; 12:22).
- Self-control is essential (Prov. 16:32; 13:3; 23:7).
- Motivate people with truth (Col. 3:23; Mk. 14:38; Mk. 1:17).
- Act financially responsible: save (Prov. 21:20); be careful of borrowing and lending money (Prov. 3:27; 17:18; 22:7).
- Receive and give correction in a proper way (Prov. 15:31; 18:19; 15:32; 2 Tim. 4:2).
- Give to God and others (Prov. 28:27; 11:24-25; 3:9-10; Gal. 6:7).
- Be equitable and just in all your dealings (Prov. 27:18; 16:2; 21:7; 14:35).
- Plan effectively (Prov. 24:3).
- Display quality leadership: be open to new ideas (Prov. 18:15); be patient (Prov. 24:10); stand up to pressure (Prov. 24:10); consider all sides of issues (Prov. 18:17).

3. A Kingdom business will offer a product or service that will be a blessing to men, and hence in harmony with God's created order.

As such, the product or service will assist in advancing God's Kingdom (government, order, rule, authority, peace) in the earth. Thus the business will not produce anything immoral or contrary to God's law, nor will it destroy man or God's moral, social, and governmental order.

4. A Kingdom business will produce financial profit; however, this is not the primary goal of Kingdom business. Rather the larger goal is to be the advancement of His Kingdom and the honor of the King.

Profitabilitiy is essential to maintain a business. A profitable business can grow, produce new jobs, and create wealth for many. Producing a financial profit is a means of blessing all those impacted by the business — the owners, the employees, the customers, the community. The profit also allows for the support of Kingdom ministry work (churches, Christian organizations, voluntary associations). Jesus praised those who returned a profit (Luke 19:11 ff). He desires us to be productive. This is part of taking dominion over the earth.

While Kingdom business will produce a profit, this is not the primary goal of Kingdom business. Rather the larger goal is to be the advancement of His Kingdom and the honor of the King. The profit generated is one means of accomplishing this (though by no way the only means), but if this becomes the primary motive of those in the business, then they have started down the wrong path that will end in undermining the business as a Kingdom business.

5. Kingdom business will demonstrate the Gospel — more so than just preaching the gospel in words — through offering an excellent good or service in a Kingdom manner. This Christian excellence and character may well open opportunities to share the Gospel message.

Advancing the Kingdom does not necessarily mean preaching the gospel in words only. In fact, for any words to have power they must be backed by character and integrity. Customers will see the character in how the business operates, and this will open opportunities to present the reason behind it.

6. Kingdom business will employ the golden rule, treating customers "with dignity and respect and not just as a means of profit."

Serving the customer is a central aspect of Kingdom business. Treating others as we would have them treat us (the golden rule) is how we love our neighbor as ourselves and one of the two great commandments.

7. Kingdom business will bless employees and cause them to grow in Christian character and a Biblical worldview.

Kingdom business recognizes that God creates people with diverse gifts. These need to be developed; plus, there should be avenues for people to apply their gifts in a constructive way. As every person contributes, the whole business will grow. Division and specialization of labor flows from this.

8. Since the business is a ministry of God it should be undergirded with prayer, and God's wisdom sought in how to daily manage all functions associated with it.

The business as a whole is a ministry of God, and each aspect of the business is a ministry as well. When problems arise, seek God for direction. Recognize that God's wisdom will come, not just through a few leaders, but through the entire business family.

9. Kingdom business runs on God's grace.

We need God's grace for all aspects of the business: for wisdom, guidance, new ideas, promotion, customers, sales, product development, etc. Our hard work alone is not enough; we also need God's grace in all things.

10. Service is the foundation for success.

Jesus set the example of servant leadership. The business leader(s) sets the example by serving God and His Kingdom purposes, serving his employees and customers, serving the shareholders, and serving his community. In turn, employees will serve all those with whom they interact.

John Wanamaker established a Kingdom business that reflected these ten characteristics, elevated mankind, and advanced God's purposes in the earth.

Criteria that Affect Business Opportunities in Nations

Before looking at Wanamaker's life, it is important to note that a nation's culture and government have a great effect upon the ability to establish Kingdom businesses in a particular nation. Without Biblical foundations in a nation, businesses will be stifled.[11] Some of the criteria that will affect business opportunities in a particular nation include:[12] degree of freedom — a nation is cultivated to the degree that it is free; degree of political stability; level of spiritual capital; level of education in the workforce; physical infrastructure; economic infrastructure; legal infrastructure; currency strength; size of domestic economy; degree of industrialization; amount of poverty. Each of these criteria should be considered when seeking to start Kingdom businesses in any particular nation.

John Wanamaker

When John Wanamaker was a boy, he went to a jewelry store in Philadelphia on a Christmas Eve to buy his mom a gift. He said, "I had only a few dollars saved up for the purpose. I wanted to buy the best thing these dollars would buy. I guess I took a long time to look at the things in the jewelry cases. The jeweler was growing impatient. Finally I said 'I'll take that,' indicating a piece — just what it was I do not recall.

"The jeweler began wrapping it up. Suddenly I saw another piece that I thought would better please my mother. 'Excuse me, sir,' I said, 'but I have changed my mind, I'll take this piece instead of the one you are wrapping.'

"You can imagine my surprise and chagrin when the jeweler answered; 'It's too late now. You've bought the first piece and you must keep it.' I was too abashed to protest. I took what I had first bought, but as I went out of the store I said to myself:

"'When I have a store of my own the people shall have what they want . . . and what they ought to have.'"[13]

This was one incident that helped create the foundation of his business.

John Wanamaker was much more than a successful merchant. He founded a new system and philosophy of business, based upon the Biblical view of man. He was a merchant pioneer who believed that "the Golden Rule of the New Testament has become the Golden Rule of business."[14] Though at times he was cynically called "Pious John" by those who thought religion had no place in business, he showed that Christianity was essential for good business.

Christianity provided the character necessary to keep the many temptations of business from blowing the merchant "over the precipice and be ruined"[15] and also the principles necessary to build a successful business. He understood stores were much more than buildings with stocks and fixtures, saying the soul of the workmen must give life to the structure, not only providing needed goods for people but "meeting the greater future of the nation" and leading "the world in its nobler civilization by its advancing education and commerce."[16]

He revolutionized business by establishing the one-price system, the money-back guarantee, the marking of the quality of goods, and the service oriented store. He was the "father of modern advertising," in that the volume of advertizing became so great as other merchants followed his lead of having daily ads in newspapers, that this gave birth to the modern newspaper and magazine, making them affordable to all.

Money did not motivate John Wanamaker to build a successful business. His desire was to serve the people. Money came as a by-product of service.

He exemplified the historical truth that capitalism is a product of Calvinism. Calvinism taught that work is an important part of Godliness; that uprightness in all one's dealing in business is required by God; that keeping account of one's dealings in business is like God keeping account of man's actions before God. It imparts a zealousness to succeed and an understanding of the importance of savings and frugality.

He had poor health (he was rejected for service in the Civil War because of this), but labored 6 days a week in the business and community, as well as every Sabbath (in teaching in the church and Sunday school) for 70 years.

He had only about two years of formal schooling, yet became one of the world's leaders in business, served in the cabinet of President Benjamin Harrison as Postmaster-General, and assisted in many voluntary associations. President Taft called him "the greatest merchant in America."[17]

Parent's Influence

John Wanamaker was born near Philadelphia in 1837 (or 1838). His mother, Elizabeth, was a devout believer who regularly taught him the *Bible*.[18] John, in his later years, wrote of the important role of his mother in his life:

> My first love was my mother and my first home was on her breast. My first bed was upon her bosom. Leaning little arms upon her knees, I learned my first prayers. A bright lamp she lit in my soul that never dies down or goes out, though the winds and waves of fourscore years have swept over me.[19]

His father worked hard, but always made time for his children. Later in life when asked where he got his inspiration to achieve so much, Wanamaker replied: "From my parents."[20]

Education and Christian Faith

From his youth he worked hard, rising at 4 a.m. for daily chores. His family had daily prayer together and often sang hymns in the evenings. From early on his greatest passion was reading, which he did all the time. He once said, "I am sure people who saw me when a boy often thought I had a tumor or some extraordinary growth where my pockets were — they were so stuffed out with books or bits of paper I had put there to study in my spare moments."[21]

Books were scarce, and his home was typical of many in that day in the books owned by the family, which included the *Bible*, *Pilgrim's Progress*, a dictionary, and *Robinson Crusoe*. Besides the *Bible*, *Robinson Crusoe* was the first book he read. Later he would give this to boys to read. John loved words, and every time he came across a new one he would look it up in the dictionary. He would at times read the dictionary for hours, storing up words like tools that he would use most effectively throughout his life.

The *Bible* was the most important book affecting his life as well as his future business. When he was eleven years old he bought his first *Bible*, what he later called "my biggest purchase."

> In a little Mission Sunday School of the Lutheran Church I bought from my teacher, Mr. Hurlbert, a small red leather Bible about eight inches long and six inches wide. This Bible cost $2.75 which I paid for in small installments as I saved up my own money that I had earned. Looking back over my life that little red Bible was the foundation on which my life has been built, and it has made possible all that had counted most in my life. I know now that it was the greatest and most important and far-reaching purchase I have ever made; and every other investment in my life seems to me, after mature years, only secondary.[22]

Wanamaker explained the great influence of that book in his life:

I believed what I read in the Bible. As a boy, so far as I know, I was not religiously inclined. But the Bible told me there was a God and how the world was created and that the attributes of God were justice, mercy, love and truth, and that injustice, selfishness, cunning, jealousies, dishonesties and falsehoods of human nature have never brought permanent success to individuals or nations.[23]

As a boy he became involved in the newly formed Sunday school. He continued to be involved in the Sunday school movement throughout his life. In 1922 he wrote to the World's Sunday School Convention, which elected him its president:

> I regard the Sunday school as the principal educator of my life. Through the Holy Scriptures I found knowledge not to be obtained elsewhere, which established and developed fixed principles and foundations upon which all I am and whatever I have done were securely built and anchored.
>
> I found faith . . . but much more I found in my Bible . . . I found the Christ, the Son of Nature but also the Son of God, endowed by His Heavenly Father with power to transform character and life. . . . I could not reject the Bible and have nothing but a human mind and other human minds to guide me, when all of us were living in bodies subject to the same temptations, passions and weaknesses of those that the Bible showed had failed, wrecked their own lives and ruined nations. . . . Faith in God casteth out fear, and courage is a fundamental Christian virtue."[24]

Christian Commitment

He was born a Methodist, attended a Lutheran Sunday school, but joined the Presbyterian Church on his own volition when he was 12 years old. One day as he walked by the Chambers Street Presbyterian Church he heard singing which drew him into the prayer meeting. He heard an old man speak of the comfort he had in his Christian faith as he approached death. John said, "That was all very well, I said to myself, but it was not what I needed. That man was at the end of his life; I was at the beginning of mine. I wanted something not to die by, but to live by."[25]

Later in the meeting a younger man arose and said he had just become a Christian and, John writes, "he wanted us to know that he was very happy in his religion, and that he had found it was the best thing in the world to live by. . . . This man was a hatter, and he said that, as he worked with his tools at his trade, somehow those very tools seemed to know that he was a Christian now."[26] This man, R.S. Walton, was later employed by Wanamaker.

"I had gotten my message," said Wanamaker, "and as the people went out from the meeting, I stayed. . . . I went up to the minister and I told him that I had settled the matter that night, and had given my heart to God."[27]

This minister, John Chambers, became a life-long friend to Wanamaker and made a great impression upon him. "I held John Chambers up as my model of righteousness," he later said in an address.[28] Wanamaker wrote down the foundations of Chamber's Christian life and sought to live by these ideals: "1. Christ demands full surrender. 2. Every follower of Christ is His messenger of good tidings. 3. Sunday is the Lord's day; it belongs to Him. 4. Alcohol is Satan's most powerful ally. 5. No man is beyond redemption."[29]

Wanamaker joined John Chamber's church and soon began to teach Sunday school, which he continued to do throughout his life. When the revival of 1857 came to Philadelphia, Wanamaker organized a Sunday night prayer meeting in his church. He taught in men's Bible classes. He became so effective in ministry that many believed he would become a preacher. He did become a preacher, though not primarily in the pulpit, but in business. He became more than a preacher in business, he became a business crusader in which he advanced God's kingdom through transforming "the business methods of the merchants of the world."[30]

Wanamaker's Occupation and Avocations

As a young man Wanamaker decided he would be a merchant. This is where his interest was and this is what he believed God called him to do. Yet, throughout his life he consistently gave himself to many areas of Christian work. He helped organize various churches and missions works, he founded and directed Sunday schools and Bible classes, and he was greatly involved in the work of the YMCA (Young Men's Christian Association). These were his avocations.

Early in his life he came to love America and appreciate the great blessings enjoyed by Americans — "We are the pride of the nations of the world!" he wrote — but expressed his concern of diminishing godliness. He said, "I sincerely believe . . . the foundation of the peace and prosperity of the land" rests upon godliness. "I feel as we cultivate holiness of heart and spread the glorious tidings of peace, inculcating the truth as it is in Jesus, so do we bind together our beloved Union. Inseparable with our prosperity is the religion of the Bible."[31] "Inseparable with our prosperity is the religion of the Bible." This was his life's creed.

Leader in the YMCA

John began working for a merchant in Philadelphia at the age of 16. After three years of non-stop labor he took an extended vacation to the mid-West to recuperate from an illness. When he returned to Philadelphia at the end of 1857, he put aside business for a time to become the first paid secretary for the YMCA, of which John had already become a member not long after the Philadelphia branch was started in 1854. This was a very difficult job as the YMCA was not yet accepted by the churches and Christian community in the area. In fact, most churches were hostile to this organization believing it detracted from their ministry. "I never worked harder in my life to stem the tide of prejudice," John later recalled.

His hard work paid off. Not only did the local YMCA grow dramatically in members, influence, and finances but it became an example to Y's all over the country as they began to hire paid secretaries and become firmly established in many cities. The name of John Wanamaker became known throughout the country. While Wanamaker went into business after three years as secretary at the YMCA, he continued to be involved in this ministry throughout his life, serving as the local president and erecting buildings as far away as India and Korea.

During these three years, the energetic Wanamaker wanted to do more than establish the YMCA, participate in revival activities, and fulfill his church and other Sunday duties, so he decided to start a Sunday school of his own. Founded in 1858, Bethany quickly became a great success. By 1908 it was the largest Sunday school in the world. Not long after the founding of Bethany Sunday school, John also founded Bethany Church. The man, which was reflected in the church, was once described by a leading minister, Dr. A.T. Pierson, as "a cross between a Presbyterian and a Methodist, with a sprinkle of independency."[32] The success of Bethany was the fruit of John's devoted Christian service. Through it "he has proved that it is possible to work a huge Christian success without forfeiting commercial prosperity; that a strong man can seek first the Kingdom and yet have all these other things also added to him."[33]

Christian work was a continual part of his life. He enjoyed it, and this is why he had seriously considered the ministry as a profession. But he believed he could be more effective in the work of God's Kingdom in business. "I would have become a minister," he said, "but the idea clung to my mind that I could accomplish more in the same domain if I became a merchant and acquired means and influence with fellow merchants."[34] Also, by applying Biblical principles in his business, he provided a great service to his fellow citizens and helped push the merchant world to adopt ideas that were a blessing to the nation.

His First Business

In February 1861, on the eve of the Civil War, Wanamaker, with partner Nathan Brown, opened a men's clothing store at Sixth and Market streets in Philadelphia. Many thought that Oak Hall Clothing would not succeed in this uncertain time, but hard work, strategic advertizing, and principles of service brought a steady increase in sales and profits. Every spare cent was put into advertizing of all sorts — billboards, posters, huge balloons, but especially newspaper ads. At this time few businesses took out ads in papers, and those that did had brief small announcements. Wanamaker pioneered a new era in newspaper advertizing. He used large displays with numerous forms of writing — from jingles to conversations of customers — to communicate the uniqueness of his business.

It was his new and unique business ideas, though, that provided the foundation for his success. These included guarantee of the quality of goods, satisfaction of the customer, items sold at a known price, and returning items for cash. *Caveat emptor, let the buyer beware*, did not apply in his store. He summarized his four cardinal points as: full guarantee, one price, cash payment, cash returned. These points were posted in ads and at his stores, as well as taught to his employees.

He tried to enlist to serve in the Union Army, but his poor health disqualified him. He found other ways to serve his country. As a means of serving the soldiers, he helped to form the Christian Commission, which was the forerunner of the Red Cross. Wanamaker was its first secretary. President Lincoln highly endorsed the new organization at an early meeting of the Commission in December 1861 in Washington, DC. It provided a great service throughout the war. Dwight L. Moody said Wanamaker was of far greater use to the nation through his work in the Christian Commission than he ever could have been as a soldier.[35] When the war ended his business began to boom.

Wanamaker's Business Principles

Wanamaker's stores stood upon principles, not profits. To him integrity, honor, and justice in business and relating to customers was of first importance. The foundation of his business success was rooted in his Christian faith and character, for these produced the principles upon which he built his successful business, which included:

- Desire to please customer: seen by returns accepted within 10 days with money back (even for custom made items)
- One set price for all
- He bought good quality items in quantity to get the lowest price, which he passed on to the customer.
- He marked the quality of the goods so the customer could know what he was getting.
- He advertized extensively and used this to educate the customer.
- He believed his service to the customer would be returned by loyalty of the customer to continue to return to buy goods.

- *The customer was right* was a foundational idea.
- At times he guaranteed a 10% lower price than anywhere else.
- He established permanent buyers in European capitals of manufacturing.

His truth in merchandising and advertizing, his straightforward dealing with customers, and the concept of service to the public laid the foundation for modern business.

Work and perseverance were central to success according to Wanamaker:

> As I grow older it becomes clearer to me that the difference between men who accomplish things and those who fail to accomplish things is in correct thinking, energy and invincible determination. A single aim and a strong spirit, undistracted and untiring, seldom fall short of the goal. Work is master key to all the doors and opportunities. The man who never quits until the work is done inevitably writes his name on the roll of winners.[36]

Pioneer in Advertizing

Wanamaker revolutionized business in many ways. He was a pioneer in the innovative use of advertizing to spread the good news of his business. He used ads to educate people in quality of goods and in how his business policies worked. He was the first person to copyright an ad. Through his daily ads he not only changed the means of attracting and educating consumers, but he also laid the foundation for the spread of newspapers to all people. Other merchants throughout America followed his example, bringing much new revenue to local papers, which enabled them to sell the papers at a price everyone could afford. He never put ads in Sunday papers, not wanting "to intrude his business in the home on the Lord's day."[37]

He was as truthful in his advertizing as he was in his personal life. Wanamaker's fundamental purpose in advertizing was, "Not to sell, but to help people to buy."[38] Thus, explaining the quality of the product was of great importance to him. People needed to know what they were getting for the price they were paying.

His success in advertizing and selling came from his character. As one magazine editor wrote: "John Wanamaker is the best advertiser in the world. He is the best advertiser because he is an honest merchant. He is an honest merchant because he is an honest man."[39]

Moody Meetings

From November 21, 1875, to January 28, 1876, Wanamaker was the major sponsor of nightly revival meetings with D.L. Moody and Ira Sankey. They met at his newly purchased depot buildings, which in 1876 became the Grand Depot Store, which was the first department store in the nation. These revival meetings were greatly successful: 10,960 people attended the opening meeting, with over one million people attending overall. Moody was the guest of Wanamaker in his home during these nine weeks.

A New Kind of Store

The Grand Depot became a new kind of store, offering not just clothing items but all kinds of products for individuals and their homes. This was the first department store in the nation. It had many new innovations:

- There was vast space with items readily displayed for customers to see.
- The store was a place to visit and enjoy without any obligation to buy.
- A large variety of goods were under one roof.
- His four points applied here as well, including one inflexible price and return of undesired purchases.
- There were free rest rooms, toilets, telegraph, and baggage check rooms.
- Employees, able to divide labor to their specialities, benefited (as did the customers) with greater wages, shorter working hours, improved work conditions with many new benefits. They also received much education in merchandising enabling them to advance upward in the business world.
- The middle man could be cut out, reducing prices.
- Advertizing revolutionized the business, and also the newspapers.
- Buildings were constructed with greater safety, better sanitation, more beauty. Many came to look at the building.
- Educational, musical, and artistic programs began to be offered regularly as a service to customers and employees. Wanamaker also encouraged his employees to play and listen to music. He wanted to make their life richer.

Department stores were a great service to the customer. Competition with smaller speciality shops prodded them into providing better goods and services. While some small shops went out of business, the number of smaller shops actually increased as Wanamaker's stores grew in size.[40] The world came to adopt his ideas.

His Stores Were a Model

John continued to expand his business and implement new ideas throughout his life. In 1911 he opened a new store in Philadelphia that was so noteworthy that President Taft dedicated it. He said that the department store that Wanamaker pioneered was "one of the most important instrumentalities in modern life for the promotion of comfort among the people,"[41] and that it would be "a model for all other stores of the same kind throughout the country and throughout the world."[42] Thirty thousand people attended this event. Words on the dedication tablet reveal the success of the Wanamaker store was due to "freedom of competition and the blessing of God."[43]

Entrepreneurs Create Jobs

Wanamaker knew from experience that excessive government laws and regulations stifle commerce and hurt businesses, small and large, as well as the overall economy. For businesses to grow, "high character," "honest industry and persistent labor" are necessary for those involved, but small taxes are just as important.[44] Thus, to Wanamaker, while the character and action of the merchant is of most importance, the government has an important role in business by limiting taxes and regulations and encouraging the free market.

At the 1911 dedication the president of the Philadelphia and Reading Railroad, George F. Baer, said:

> We live in an age which is peculiarly tending toward socialism in all its ugliest features, socialism based upon the old fallacy that all men are equal if they be given the same opportunity, a fallacy whose falsity is demonstrated here today. Fifty years ago there were thousands of people who had the same opportunity as our distinguished host. He was the architect of his own fortune. Thousands upon thousands saw opportunity pass by day after day without the ability or courage to seize it. This world's work is, and always must be, controlled and governed by a few superior men who have the courage to say in business and everywhere else what our honored President said, 'I will find a way or make it.[45]

Merchant Pioneer

Wanamaker pioneered many things in business. (Some are listed above.) Others include:

- His was the first store to be lighted by electricity in 1878.
- His was the first store in Philadelphia to utilize the telephone (1879).
- He sought to continually reduce prices by buying in large volumes and passing on savings to the customer. He explained this in his advertizing.
- He passed on benefits to the employees from increased sales.
- To support the country, he kept his employees who enlisted in the Spanish-American war on full pay.
- He was always helping victims of natural disasters (floods, earthquakes, famine, etc.) by collecting supplies and money at his stores to pass on to those in need in the USA and other countries. These efforts assisted Native Americans, blacks, and women in many ways. He formed the Red, White and Blue Cross to enable his employees to serve those in need.
- He opened medical offices in his stores for his employees.
- He regularly educated his employees.
- He built a bicycle factory to make this means of transportation affordable to everyone.

- He carried Ford cars in his stores, offering them at a lower price than other dealers, and helped to lay the foundation for the success of Ford Motor Company.
- Wanamaker's was the first store to display and sell an airplane in 1909. His store was also the first to have a department for selling commercial planes (1925). In 1926 the store also displayed Richard Byrd's plane that flew over the North Pole.
- He opened Marconi Wireless stations in his stores in 1911 where people could send messages through the air.
- He set up a retirement plan for his employees.
- He promoted women in business, and his stores had much to do with their progress.
- He established recreation clubs for his employees.
- He provided many musical opportunities for his employees and performances in his stores for the general public.

He applied the Golden Rule to employees and customers. He promoted better working conditions — including less work hours per week, retirement plans, medical plans, better work environment (with lockers, cafeterias, recreation clubs) — and operated with the view that all his employees were part of the Wanamaker family. With both customers and employees in view, he pioneered store comforts: heat and ventilation, elevators, electric lights, and ease of access.

His Philadelphia store became the largest in the world. It was much more than just its physical size. It had a spirit, a personality. The employee sought to serve the customer and had his well-being in mind. The store entertained, educated, and performed special services. People enjoyed visiting, whether they bought items or not, and were refreshed from the visit. Universities studied his stores to learn successful economic principles. They could see them at work. His success came from his character.

Wanamaker said, "Commerce . . . is the very life blood that pulsates through every fibre of a healthy body politic."[46] What Wall Street or investment banks did was of no matter unless commerce was full of life and advancing.

He believed strongly in the free market and individual enterprise, with government involved only in keeping the market free and fair. The best means of advancing the economy and producing the growth of business in a nation was to keep taxes low, cut government regulations, and encourage competition. "Business thrives on competition," he wrote, "and that the people's interests in getting better merchandise and lower prices are always improved when competition is unstifled!"[47]

Conducted His Business with Integrity and Christian Character

His business integrity was consistent throughout his life. During WWI he refused to increase his prices even though a diminishing supply of goods was forcing the prices up on many goods throughout the country.

He exemplified great character himself. He was an indefatigable worker — managing all aspects of his business, having knowledge of and giving oversight to many areas. He wrote his own business editorials which contained much wisdom on many things. He replied to every personal letter sent to him. He was always punctual and was one of the first to arrive at the store.

Work

He believed each man had the capacity within himself to be successful, but this required work. "Success lies less in the possession of some special gift," he said, "than it lies in the human power to put to use the more or less common gifts of which almost every one has absolute ownership." "The first step toward success in any vocation is a willingness to work."[48]

He believed those people who created opportunities for other men to work and earn money deserved a crown, because "what men want most is something to do." Wanamaker wrote, "Men who furnish work for their fellow men are the men who invest capital for the benefit of the human race."[49]

Save

His personal character laid the foundation for a successful business. He kept his priorities in order, displayed Biblical character qualities of personal conduct, sought to serve God and man, and also acted in a way necessary to succeed in business. Early on he learned the necessity of making and saving money. Born without fortune, he learned the importance of hard work and frugality. "Thrift, he said, "is one of the foundation stones of character." To succeed men must save. "The way to save is to begin at once." This indicates that a young man or young woman "intend to try and succeed on their own efforts, and not depend on others for their success."[50] His first savings of seven cents came out of money he made working in his father's brickyard. Of riches he wrote: "There is no harm in being rich, if the rich man's spirit is right."[51]

Business as a Ministry

Throughout his life, John Wanamaker supported much Christian work: his first church, Bethany Sunday School, Bethany Church, the YMCA, the Salvation Army, Moody meetings, and many other Christian endeavors all over the world. Moreover, Wanamaker saw his business as a ministry through which he sought to serve and bless men, as well as to advance God's Kingdom. His mother wanted him to become a clergyman. He did the work of a minister throughout his life (at Bethany and various ministries), but he felt he could do more for God's kingdom through business than full-time in the pulpit. He said, "I could accomplish more in the same domain if I became a merchant and acquired means and influence."[52] He kept a proper perspective of his business work and other Kingdom work. He saw "religion first, earning power next, and a vision of general culture later."[53]

He wrote: "There is nothing in this world that has given me the satisfaction that the time spent in the service of God and His people has given me. The things of this world pass away, but the things of God are eternal."[54]

Service to Country

John showed his love for America in many ways. For example, he supported the effort of the U.S.A. in WWI: Wanamaker continued the salaries and preserved the jobs of the men from his stores who went to fight in WWI; he organized military training for men in his stores; he issued Liberty Bonds, himself buying $35 million of them, on which he lost over two million dollars.

Wanamaker loved his God and his country. The Bible and the American flag were symbols of his life. He wrote on Flag Day in 1919: "The American Flag is bigger than any territory, more powerful than any political party, and its principles link it to a religion of duty and life broader than any creed. To love it and be for what it stands is next to the love of God."[55]

John served as the Postmaster-General during Benjamin Harrison's administration. Under his leadership the postal service advanced greatly. This was due to his character and business skills. He acted against political corruption, refusing to make political appointments, and he sought to run the postal service like a business.

He was involved in politics during much of his life — he served in the Harrison administration, he ran for the U.S. senate and for governor, and he fought against the corrupt political machine in Pennsylvania — what he called the "cesspools of Quay politics." When he was defeated in his run for senator, he wrote that it was providential because had he won he would have never taken up the battle against the machine.[56]

Throughout his sixty plus years in business he faced many difficult times, some brought on by economic downturns in the nation. In these trying times Wanamaker looked to God for strength. He wrote in his diary on November 7, 1907, during one of those national economic crises when many men had lost their fortunes and "great men's hearts" were "quaking with fear": "The truth is that there is but one, the Holy One Himself, who can still this storm and calm the tumultuous waters. I am learning to pray and am looking to the Father above for light and help, not altogether for the business, but to give me health and wisdom and to make me able to cope with circumstances as they arise."[57]

Wanamaker did much more than supply goods and services to his fellow man. He ministered to men, by not only raising their standard of living, but also by bringing art, culture, and a new outlook on life. He transformed the cultural and spiritual environment of many. He led the way in changing the environment of business in America — he elevated those who worked for him, men and women; he established justice in every transaction, providing the excellent quality of goods in his stores that he advertized; he built his stores upon honor and truthfulness.

Wanamaker had a Christian view of man. He believed God made each person for a purpose and equipped him to succeed, but each man has a part to play in his success; thus some succeed and some do not. Speaking to students at Pierce Business School of Philadelphia he said:

> I think it is possible for you to succeed, because we came out from God, the source of life, to do something He fitted us for in the world He made for man, and the life He gave to each must go back to Him to give account of what the man did with it. I do not think He made us in His own image and likeness without meaning to help us to success, and we must admit the Creator surely has a right to elect His own way to do His work.[58]

He saw that God created the world and placed man in it to take dominion over His creation. He believed that God gave man the capacity to work with Him to bring advancement in all areas of life. "Life is indeed a beautiful thing," he wrote. "The world is unfinished. We are here to play our part in it. We want to make the best of our own lives."[59]

In 1917 he wrote that "a man's character is generally formed in the first 20 years of his life." He pointed out how various external things shape a man's character — education, associations, environment — but that which is within a man is of most consequence — his own will, his clear view of right and wrong, his moral courage. Of most importance in shaping the inward man "is an unswerving belief in the inspired word of God and in the value of his own soul."[60]

Wanamaker's Christian faith was central to his life and success as a businessman. He looked to God's Word as the foundation for his character and worldview, writing in 1922:

> What good is there in rejecting the Bible? — A mere abstract belief that God exists is not of much practical value. I found in my Bible the Christ, the Son of nature but also the Son of God — whoever will do what Christ tells him will find faith and freedom and power in trying to imitate Him, and by prayer to the Father, in His Name, will be wonderfully helped to live his life and do things that will benefit the world.[61]

He always kept a small Bible in his pocket. He would often read from its well-worn pages passages to comfort those in sorrow and encourage those in need.

His humility is seen as he wrote in his later years looking back over his life — a life full of productivity which extended God's kingdom greatly and advanced men throughout the world: "The only wish I have is that I could have done all my work better."[62]

Throughout his life when others acclaimed him and his works, Wanamaker would turn to the ultimate source of his success and say as he did in laying the capstone of the new Philadelphia building, June 11, 1910:

> I want to say, first of all, that one Hand alone has made it possible for us to have this day of felicity. That one Hand planted the forests, built into the hills the stone, laid down deep in the earth the iron, and through all the fifty years — beautiful years of dreaming and daring, but of health and of hope, of struggles and schooling, years the history of which it would be hard to write — plainly written over all these years, guiding and guarding, is the one signature of the good God, who is interested in us not only on Sundays, but on week days — the Father of us all, who cares for what we are doing. I want to say to the younger people coming on that it is poor prosperity that is blind to the need of God's favor, whether we are in business or out of it.[63]

Wanamaker died in the harness, in that he continued working to the last months of his life. His last active day in the office was September 19, 1922, age 84. He worked all day in the New York store and returned late to his home near Philadelphia. He went to his Philadelphia office the next day, but was very tired and weak. His doctor saw him and ordered him home, which he reluctantly obeyed. He never returned to his office, though he attempted to continue to write business editorials at home. He could not write long as he gradually grew weaker. He died on December 12, 1922.

The Most Influential Layman of the Protestant Church

At a memorial service for John Wanamaker, Dr. MacLennan said, "The world has lost one of its outstanding men, not of one generation, but of many generations."[64] Bishop Berry commented: "He was probably the most influential layman of the Protestant Church. His life speaks to us of his ardent love for the Bible, of his loyalty to the Christian Sabbath, of his practical interest in every moral reform. His public life was as true to Christian standards as was his life in business or at home."[65]

The capstone of his new store of 1910 was inscribed: "Let those who follow me continue to build with the plumb of Honor, the level of Truth, and the square of Integrity, Education, Courtesy and Mutuality."[66]

While Wanamaker was in a competitive business, and many opposed him, his Christian character won over even his enemies. At a New York merchants dinner given in Wanamaker's honor in 1911, the view of most merchants was expressed in a speech: "Here is a man who has spent fifty years in a competitive business, and he has made of his competitors not enemies, but friends and admirers."[67]

William Jennings Bryan called him "America's greatest merchant . . . illustrating the possibilities in this land of the free . . . his political career illustrates a high type of citizenship — he takes time for patriotic duties . . . his personal life illustrates the beauty of Christian service."[68] Industry, undergirded by integrity, justice, morality, and fair dealings produced "the greatest merchant in all the world."[69]

In response to a request for a sketch of his life, Wanamaker replied laconically: "Thinking, trying, toiling, and trusting in God is all of my biography."[70]

The Provost of the University of Pennsylvania summarized Wanamaker's work when he conferred upon him the Doctor of Laws degree: "Philanthropist, Statesman, eminent in the councils of the nation, Christian leader, constructive genius who on the basis of the Golden Rule by thought and practice has revolutionized the business methods of the merchants of the world."[71]

Joseph Lister and John Wanamaker transformed medicine and business by applying Biblical principles in their divine occupations. There have been many other Christians who have done similar things in all spheres of life by multiplying and utilizing the talents and skills that God gave them with the view of advancing His Kingdom and bringing Him glory. Others who applied Biblical principles in the marketplace include: Johann Gutenberg and Samuel F.B. Morse (invention), Matthew Fontaine Maury (discovery), Michael Faraday (technology), Noah Webster (education), Christopher Columbus (exploration), Isaac Newton (science), George Washington Carver (agriculture), and Cyrus McCormick (invention and business).[72]

Most Christians are not called to the pulpit ministry; rather most Christians are called to the marketplace. They need to understand that their occupation is a ministry where they are to glorify God, serve their fellow man, and advance Christ's Kingdom. Crawford W. Long, developer of anesthetics for surgery, reflected this understanding declaring: **"My profession is to me a ministry of God."**[73]

Kingdom businesses and our calling in the marketplace are a key part of our taking dominion over the earth. This has been God's charge to man from the beginning. As each of us fulfills our Kingdom purpose (in our occupational calling, as well as in our responsibilities in the family, church, and state) we will all contribute to the march of His Kingdom in history. *PP*

End Notes

1. Laurence Farmer, *Master Surgeon, A Biography of Joseph Lister*, New York: Harper & Row, 1962, pp. 28-29.

2. See Luke 19:11-27, the parable of the minas, and further explanation in Stephen McDowell, *Building Godly Nations,* Charlottesville, Vir.: Providence Foundation, 2004, Chapters 1, 3.

3. Farmer, p. 34.

4. Farmer, p. 45.

5. Farmer, p. 46.

6. Farmer, p. 121.

7. Farmer, p. 115.

8. For other examples, see *Building Godly Nations*, especially Chapter 1 and 14; *America's Providential History*; *In God We Trust Tour Guide*, Section 3 (on William Penn); and past *Providential Perspectives* on Matthew Fontaine Maury and Marcus and Narcissa Whitman.

9. Ken Eldred, *God Is at Work*, Ventura, Cal.: Regal Books, 2005, p. 60. For another great example of a Kingdom businessman see "Biblical Principles of Business — Exemplified by Cyrus McCormick," in *Building Godly Nations*, Chapter 14.

10. Ideas for these from Paul Stevens in Eldred, pp. 62-65.

11. Biblical economic ideas are covered in other books and courses offered by the Providence Foundation Biblical Worldview University. Books: *Liberating the Nations*, Chapter 12, "Principles of Christian Economics;" *Building Godly Nations*, Chapter 14; *The Economy from a Biblical Perspective*. BWU Courses: *Biblical Economics, Business, & the Marketplace* and *Principles for Transforming the Marketplace.*

12. Eldred, pp. 172-173.

13. Joseph H. Appel, *The Business Biography of John Wanamaker, Founder and Builder*, New York: The Macmillan Company, 1930.

14. *Ibid.*, p. xv.

15. *Ibid.*, p. xv.

16. *Ibid.*, p. viii.

17. *Ibid.*, p. xvi.

18. *Ibid.*, p. 9.

19. *Ibid.*, p. 10.

20. *Ibid.*, p. 11.

21. *Ibid.*, p. 15.

22. *Ibid.*, p. 16-17.

23. *Ibid.*, p. 17.

24. *Ibid.*, p. 22.

25. *Ibid.*, p. 23.

26. *Ibid.*, p. 23.

27. *Ibid.*, p. 23.

28. *Ibid.*, p. 23.

29. *Ibid.*, p. 24.

30. *Ibid.*, p. 118.

31. *Ibid.*, p. 30-31.

32. *John Wanamaker*, Herbert Adams Gibbons, in Two Volumes, New York: Harper & Brothers Pub., 1926, 1:193.

33. Appel, p. 36.

34. *Ibid.*, p. 39.

35. *Ibid.*, p. 51.

36. *Ibid.*, p. 194.

37. *Ibid.*, p. 307.

38. *Ibid.*, p. 397.

39. *Ibid.*, p. 131.

40. *Ibid.*, p. 111.

41. *Ibid.*, p. 205.

42. *Ibid.*, p. 206.

43. *Ibid.*, p. 208.

44. *Ibid.*, p. 216.

45. *Ibid.*, p. 219.

46. *Ibid.*, p. 197.

47. *Ibid.*, p. 291.

48. *Ibid.*, p. 337.

49. *Ibid.*, p. 338.

50. *Ibid.*, p. 323.

51. *Ibid.*, p. 329.

52. *Ibid.*, p. 323.

53. *Ibid.*, p. 322.

54. *Ibid.*, p. 322.

55. *Ibid.*, p. 308.

56. *Ibid.*, p. 321.
57. *Ibid.*, p. 150.
58. *Ibid.*, p. 340.
59. *Ibid.*, p. 285.
60. *Ibid.*, p. 340-341.
61. *Ibid.*, p. 352.
62. *Ibid.*, p. 353.
63. *Ibid.*, p. 437.
64. *Ibid.*, p. 360.
65. *Ibid.*, p. 360.
66. *Ibid.*, p. 115.
67. *Ibid.*, p. 126.
68. *Ibid.*, p. 280.
69. *Ibid.*, p. 281.
70. *Ibid.*, p. 224.

71. *Ibid.*, p. 117-118.
72. See *Building Godly Nations* by Stephen McDowell for more on some of these men, as well as other Christians who have advanced God's Kingdom in all spheres of life.
73. A statue of Long with this inscription is displayed in the United States Capitol Building.

* * *

Copies of this booklet can be ordered from the Providence Foundation for $6.95 each. Use the order form on the last page, visit our website (www.providencefoundation.com), or call 434-978-4535.

Biblical Worldview University

Training leaders of education, business, and politics to transform their culture for Christ.

The Biblical Worldview University (BWU) provides training for leaders of all ages and spheres of life in a curriculum of real-world topics, offered via distance learning and periodic live classes. BWU offers dozens of courses under five general areas of study. A few courses are listed below. Start your Biblical worldview training today by ordering one or more of the following courses. The prices are for auditing the classes. To enroll for credit ask for an enrollment form. For a complete list of courses see our website or request a catalog (email: university@providencefoundation.com; phone: 434-978-4535).

Order online: www.providencefoundation.com (or use form on last page)

General Biblical Worldview
1. Fundamentals for Biblical Transformation . . . Audit Cost: $50
2. Providential World History: The Chain of Liberty . . . Audit Cost: $80

Providential History
1. America's Christian History (Vision and Planting) . . . Audit Cost: $80
2. America's Christian History (Beginning and Growth) . . . Audit Cost: $80

The Family and Christian Education
1. Christian Education and Biblical Worldview . . . Audit Cost: $90

The Marketplace — Business, Economics, and Finance
1. Foundations of Biblical Economics, Business, & Marketplace . . . Audit Cost: $45
2. Principles for Transforming the Marketplace . . . Audit: $60

The State — Government, Law, and Political Science
1. God and Government . . . Audit Cost: $40.

Response & Order Form

I want to join the Providence Foundation by becoming:

☐ **BASIC MEMBER**: those who contribute $120 or more per year receive our newsletters, a 30% discount on all our books, videos, and materials, plus discounts to our seminars. Enclosed is my gift of:

$ _____

☐ **PREMIUM MEMBER**: those who contribute $588 ($120 to start, $39/month) or more per year receive Basic Member benefits plus a free book, $80 voucher toward one of our Biblical Worldview University Courses, personal coaching, and more. I will send a regular gift of $_____ per month / qrtr / year (circle one). Enclosed is my gift of:

$ _____

☐ **SUPPORTER**: those who contribute any amount toward the ongoing ministry of the Providence Foundation receive the *Reformation Report* and other mailings. Enclosed is my gift of:

$ _____

I wish to order the following items:

Qty	Title/Product code	Price	Total

	Subtotal	
	Member discount (30%)	
Shipping & Handling : * U.S. Mail: $4.00 minimum, 10% if over $40 * UPS: $5.50 minimum, 12% if over $50.	Sales tax (VA orders add 5%)	
	Shipping	
	TOTAL	
	Contribution	
☐ Please send me a Resource Catalog	**GRAND TOTAL**	

Method of Payment: ☐ Check/M.O. ☐ VISA ☐ MC ☐ AmEx ☐ Cash

For Membership: I request my bank or credit card company to monthly transfer funds in the amount of $_____ until further notice. I prefer a monthly transfer date of the 5th or the 20th (circle one) starting _____ (month). ☐ **Checking** (Attach a voided check) ☐ **Savings** (Attach a voided deposit ticket)

Credit Card No.:_____ Exp. date: _____

Signature:_____

SHIP TO:

Name:_____

Address:_____

City:_____ State:____ Zip:_____

Phone:(____)_____

Email:_____

Make checks payable to:
Providence Foundation
PO Box 6759
Charlottesville, VA 22906
Phone: 434-978-4535

Also, order by phone or at website
www.providencefoundation.com